Deirdre and the Sons of Uisneach

A Scoto-Irish Romance Of
The First Century A.D

William Graham

Alpha Editions

This Edition Published in 2020

ISBN: 9789354215421

Design and Setting By
Alpha Editions
www.alphaedis.com
Email – info@alphaedis.com

As per information held with us this book is in Public Domain.
This book is a reproduction of an important historical work. Alpha Editions uses the best technology to reproduce historical work in the same manner it was first published to preserve its original nature. Any marks or number seen are left intentionally to preserve its true form.

PREFACE

THE larger portion of the following compilation was read to the Glasgow Bankers' Debating and Literary Society in December last, and has been allowed to retain much of its original form, with the addition of some explanatory notes, where these seemed necessary.

The previous month of September had been spent at Ledaig, near Oban, where, as a holiday task, the writer learned something of the history of the clan commemorated in the neighbouring vitrified Fort of the Sons of Uisneach. Subsequent research showed how widely their story was known to Celtic scholarship, and in what various forms it had already been published. To the general reader, however, as ignorant of Gaelic as the present writer, the story may serve as an introduction to the comparatively unknown, but wonderfully interesting, field of ancient Celtic literature, and it is to the general reader alone that these notes are now offered. They contain nothing for the scholar, unless matter for criticism and correction.

Just as these pages were ready for the press, two notable additions to the Uisneach literature appeared, both from the hands of eminent Celtic scholars. Professor MacKinnon, of the Celtic Chair in Edinburgh University, has concluded an able translation of the Glenmasan MS. in the Advocates' Library, Edinburgh. This MS. bears date 1238 A.D., but Professor MacKinnon considers it cannot be placed earlier than the end of the fifteenth century. He adds, however, that " the existing copy may well have been transcribed from an older MS., whose date was 1238 A.D. The writer of the note [as to the date] had authority of some kind when he is so specific as to the day and year. One may go further and say that the contents of our MS. were reduced to writing long before 1238 A.D. The Glenmasan MS. must have undergone several recensions before the existing copy was made."

The other work referred to is a literal translation by Mr Alexander Carmichael of the story of "Deirdire and the Lay of the Children of Uisné" as orally collected on the Island of Barra. The fact that this tale should have lingered on in tradition for so many centuries amid the solitudes of the Outer Hebrides, and yet be found presenting the same general features as in the Edinburgh MS. of 1500 or the Irish books of 1100 or 1150, affords a singular evidence of the extraordinary interest attaching to the central figures of the tragedy, " Uisné's Children of the White Horses," and of Deirdre of Erinn, the Darthula of Alban, the most beautiful woman of Irish antiquity, " whose locks were more yellow than the western gold of the summer sun."

The *Celtic Review*, for which Professor MacKinnon is consulting editor, will be found a mine of accurate information on the ancient history and literature of the Celtic world, and a perusal of a few of its numbers will convince the most stolid Saxon of the debt which the world owes to the genius and energy of the Celtic races. To still further awaken interest in these subjects is the strong desire of the present writer.

EDINBURGH, *March* 1908.

CONTENTS

CHAPTER I
	PAGE
Introduction	11

CHAPTER II

Loch Etive — Benderloch — Beregonium — Dun Mac Uisneach — Hector Boece — Dean of Lismore's Book — Bibliography of the Story 16

CHAPTER III

The Hill of Usnagh — Three Sorrowful Tales — King Lir — King Tuathal — Three Ancient MSS. 20

CHAPTER IV

The Uisneachs' Birth and Education — Skye — Conor Macnessa — Birth of Deirdre — Caffa the Druid — Deirdre's Wooing — Flight to Scotland 29

CHAPTER V

Loch Etive — Deirdre's First Home — Dun Mac Uisneach — Remains of the Fort — Clach Manessa — Eilean Uisneachan — Deirdre's Drawing-room — Her Children — Adventures at Inverness — Dunadd and Duntroon Castle — Scottish Scenery — Recalled to Ireland — Deirdre's Lament 40

CHAPTER VI

Landing in Ireland—The Traitor Borach—Arrival at Emania—Siege of the Red Branch House—The Sortie, Surrender, and Massacre of the Uisneachs—Deirdre a Captive—Eoghan Mac Durrthacht—Deirdre's Death 60

CHAPTER VII

The Origin and Building of Emania—Macha Red Hair—King Fergus Mac Roigh's Death—Queen Meav of Cruachan—Conor Macnessa's last Days and Death 74

DEIRDRE AND THE SONS OF UISNEACH

CHAPTER I

INTRODUCTION

FOR some time prior to the summer of 1907 the writer had been interested in the connection existing in ancient times between the Gaelic-speaking peoples of Ireland and of Alban (Scotland).

The historical records of this connection are few and brief until the coming of the Dalriadic Scots to Argyleshire, but, apart from historic evidence, its existence is amply proved by the great fact of a common language, which has left its indelible mark on the place-names of both nations.

In every direction north and west of the Scottish Highland Line, where the spoken tongue (after allowance for dialectical changes) is still the same as in Ancient Ireland, we are not surprised to find that Celtic names survive similar in form to those which mark the scenery of Old Ireland. Beautiful

Kintail, at the head of Loch Duich in Wester Ross, is the same as Kintale in Killygarvan parish, Donegal, or Kinsale in Cork, all three being "The head of the brine," marking as they do the limit of the salt water at or near the top of sea lochs. There are Kin-ards (high heads) in Ireland as in Scotland, though the meaning of the Scottish headland near Fraserburgh is obscured by the absurd map-title "Kinnaird's Head"! The "Bals"[1] of Scotland are the "Ballys"[2] of Ireland, from the common root, "Baile," a town.

Hundreds of Ards, or Duns, or Bens[3] are common to both countries, and the Auchs or Achs[4] of Alban are the Aghs or Aughs of Erinn.

But it is doubly interesting to observe how even in the south and east of Scotland, where Saxon or Scandinavian peoples have settled to the utter extinction of Celtic as a current language, centuries of such domination have failed to touch the vast majority of the chief place-names. They remain as purely Celtic as in Wales, Donegal, or Galway. The

---

[1] *e.g.* Balquhidder, Balmoral, or Ballinluig.
[2] Ballyshannon, Ballycastle.
[3] Heights, or hills, or mountains.
[4] Auch, Ach, Agh, Augh = "Field," *e.g.* Auchterarder, Auchnasheen, Aghamore, or Aughnahoy.

southern river systems are almost wholly Celtic; witness the Clyde, the Tweed, the Annan, and the Nith, or the smaller waters of the Esks, the Almond, and the Avon, the Ettrick, the Teviot, and the Tyne, the Dee, the Ken, and the Cree, or the "bonny Doon" or Water of Ayr. The Pentland Hills mark the southern boundary, as the Pentland Firth marks the northern, of the land of the Pehts or Picts, a purely Celtic people at continual war with the British Celts further south. From Duns to Dumbarton, from Dalkeith to Dalbeattie, from Dunfermline to Dumfries the old names remain Celtic, even though the last named indicates an incursion of Frisans. Aberdeen, with its Dee and Don,[1] Dundee and its Tay, Fife, Leith, Innerleithen, Peebles, Galashiels, or Melrose, and last, and greatest, Glasgow, all tell the same tale. They are the names given to places in the dim past of Alban by its Celtic people, whose language in Eastern and Southern Scotland has perished as a spoken tongue.

The present inhabitants of Lowland Scotland, though with much admixture of other blood in the

---

[1] Both rivers probably included in its name Aber,—Dee—[DO]N, the "D" being lost first, in vocalisation, and the vowel sound O soon following it.

eastern districts, are the undoubted descendants of these prehistoric clans, with many purely Celtic words in their Lowland speech and song to remind them of the ancient race; but otherwise, save for some solitary battle-stone or lonely cairn, that race is as forgotten as the forest leaves which covered their graves.

With so great a weight of linguistic evidence, and so little in comparison from strictly historic sources, any surviving word of literature which remains to tell something of these far off-days, of the ancestry of the peoples of Scotland, of the land the Scots came from, of the scenery of wood and mountain of the land they invaded and gave their name to, becomes profoundly interesting. The dry bones of the Antiquarian Museum shake themselves into human form and come forth into the sunlight to speak with us face to face. The relics of archæology are precious, but too often they are dumb, and compared with them, the survivals of literature give us the flash of the human eye, the sound of the human voice, and the thoughts of the mind across a bridge of twenty centuries.

In this story of Deirdre and the Sons of Uisneach we have such a "surviving word" which has come down through nineteen hundred years. For its leading facts we have to thank these eminent Celtic scholars whose labours have done so much in tracing out the beginnings of our race. The story is known in various forms in Ireland, in the Highlands of Scotland, and in the Outer Hebrides. It has been published in part, and even in considerable detail, at various times, but, so far as known to the writer, the full narrative, embracing the wanderings of the heroes in Scotland (Alban), has not previously been made public in a united and popular form. Being ignorant of the Celtic language, the writer has been dependent on the labours of others for translations, but he has followed safe guides, and has sought to make due acknowledgment of these in the narrative.

To the many visitors to Oban, Loch Etive, and Glen Etive, or the village of Ledaig, the story will give a new interest in their travels.

CHAPTER II

Loch Etive — Benderloch — Beregonium — Dun Mac Uisneach — Hector Boece — Dean of Lismore's Book — Bibliography of the Story.

THERE must be few tourists in Scotland who do not know Connel Ferry Junction, the last station on the Callander and Oban Railway before it runs down the long loop into Oban.

From the Junction a new railway line crosses the mouth of Loch Etive at the Falls of Lora, and after running for two miles with the Bay of Ard-na-Muich (The Hill of the Boar) on the left, and the beautiful Ach-na-Cree Moss on the right, the train passes under the huge cliff of Dunvalanree, the Fort of the King's House, and stops at Benderloch Station. Benderloch is really the name of the parish, an irregular peninsula between Loch Etive on the south and Loch Creran on the north. The village near the station is called Ledaig, but was formerly called Keills or Cills (the church), whose very ancient church (of which a few foundation stones remain in the old graveyard) was possibly consecrated by St Columba or one of his early successors.

Immediately to the west of the station there lies a long dark hillock or dun, about 250 or 300 yards from north to south, and about 50 feet in height, lying like a huge leech on the green meadow, ringed round by low precipices, save where the walls of rock are pierced by grassy slopes. The sea end of the hill faces south, falling sharply to the northern shore of Ard-na-Muich Bay, and commanding a glorious expanse of the Morven hills and mountains of Mull to the west.

Southward lies Dunstaffnage Castle, three miles off, backed by the endless hills round Oban, while to the east rise the crags of Ben Lora, looking down on the supposed scene of many an Ossianic legend.

The guide-books, misled, alas! by the Ordnance Survey maps, say that this hillock is *Beregonium*, the capital of the ancient kingdom of the Picts, and that it was destroyed by fire from heaven! James Hogg, the Ettrick Shepherd, visited the spot and swallowed the *Beregonium* delusion like the man and the poet he was. There were no critics in his day to ask every tale for the faith to be put in it. Hogg came home to St Mary's Loch and wrote his poem, "Queen

Hynde," incorporating the legend of fire from heaven and mingling the characters of eight centuries in picturesque anachronism.

On inquiry it was disappointing to find that the grand-sounding name *Beregonium* was a mere mediæval invention, unknown in history until Hector Boece, in his Latin History of Scotland (1527), located an imaginary King Fergus in a castle of this name at Lough-quabre (Lochaber). He was probably misled by using a copy of Ptolemy, published at Ulm in 1486, in which, by misprint, Beregonium appears in place of Rerigonium at Loch Ryan. Boece located Ptolemy's places many miles to the north of their correct position. Some later imaginative writer—probably Buchanan, who writes of "Bergon"—drafted Lochaber twenty miles southward and fixed the name *Beregonium* to our dun at Ledaig, where it has since stood in the guide-books, though happily not to the oblivion of the true name of this very ancient and interesting site, DUN MHIC UISNEACH, *i.e.* the Fort of the Sons of Uisneach, and the reader may at once ask who were the sons of Uisneach, and who or where was Uisneach?

Perusal of Dr Angus Smith's interesting book on "Loch Etive and the Sons of Uisneach," followed by consultation of Mr W. F. Skene's "Celtic Scotland," and the same author's Introduction to the printed edition of "The Dean of Lismore's Book" shewed where to look for material, and the writer is indebted above all to Professor Eugène O'Curry's "MS. Materials of Irish History," and his contribution on this story to the *Atlantis Magazine*. Another treasure was found in Dr Joyce's work on Irish place-names, and in his "Old Celtic Romances," where the Uisneach story is told. These, with numerous minor references, supplied what follows.

CHAPTER III

The Hill of Usnagh—Three Sorrowful Tales—King Lir—King Tuathal—Three Ancient MSS.

LEGEND and tradition tell that for centuries before Christianity entered Ireland (St Patrick began his mission there in 432 A.D.) the sacred druidic hill of Uisneach, now the Hill of Usnagh, or Usny, in the parish of Conry in West Meath, a few miles west from Mullingar, had been regarded as the religious centre of Erinn, as it was also the geographical centre. On it the sacred Beltane fires had burned, until as a site it was robbed of part of its sanctity by having to share its honours with other three sites at the will of the great Scotic conqueror, King Tuathal Techtmar or The Acceptable. This possibly was done for political reasons, to minimise the affection for the old site, Tuathal being the head of an invading and conquering race, reigning on to A.D. 160 or thereby. Though essentially pagan in its celebrations, the regard for Usnagh held on into Christian times, and so late as " 1111 A.D. the Synod of Uisneach met with fifty bishops, three hundred priests, and three thousand ecclesiastics." These facts throw some light on the almost supernatural regard with which these children of Uisneach were viewed. Much of the sanctity of their place of origin must have attached to their persons as descended from the race of the Druids, and their terrible death was evidently resented by their people not merely on account of the treachery which accompanied it, but on account of its sacrilegious character.

Possibly Uisneach was originally a person, but such personality, if it ever existed, is absolutely lost in the dim past, unless it survives in the name of Ireland's sacred hill.

Turning from geography to letters, the ancient literature of Ireland contains three great tragedies which stand out in a rank by themselves. They are collectively called "The Three Most Sorrowful of Story Telling of Erinn," The "Tri Thruaighe na Scealaigheachta."

We shall find ourselves among the highest pinnacles of literature if we believe that the second of these, "The Tragedy of the Children of Lir," or Lér (the Neptune of pagan Erinn), is, as supposed, the original on which Shakespeare founded his immortal "King

Lear." There are, however, few resemblances in the two tales, save a very sorrowful father in both. Lir's four children combine to make one gentle patient Cordelia, and in the Irish tale there is one fearful woman, before whom even Regan and Goneril must quail. It is nevertheless worth noting that the old romance of Lir's son Manannan is common to the Welsh as well as to Ireland, having been carried to North Wales in the early invasions by the Scots from Ulster. The Isle of Man is called after this hero, also possibly Slamannan (Slieve Mannan) in Scotland, and Clackmannan, a few miles farther north. These names mean respectively the District and Stone of Mannan. As Shakespeare was born on the Welsh border it is probable he was acquainted with these Celtic legends. He gives Iona its true ancient name of Colmekill when recording the burial of Duncan in "Macbeth," and his Queen Mab in "A Midsummer Night's Dream" is an Irish lady to whom reference is made later. Matthew Arnold and J. R. Green both refer in classic sentences to the manifestation of the Celtic spirit in Shakespeare's finest work; while Professor Morley ventures to say, "But for the early, pregnant, and continuous contact with the race that in its half barbaric days invented 'Ossian's Dialogue with St Patrick,'

Germanic England would not have produced Shakespeare." The third of the "Three Sorrowful Tales" is that of the children of Tuireann, a story of the feuds between the Fomorians (a race of sea-pirates) and the Dedannan or predecessors of the Milesian (Scotic) race, after which we come to what is probably the earliest in point of composition of these three famous tales, viz.—

THE EXILE AND SORROWS OF THE CHILDREN OF UISNEACH. Their story as told in the Irish annals is so ancient that one hesitates before asking readers to believe that its characters lived and died about the time of our Saviour's crucifixion, and it is because in this undoubtedly very ancient tale that we first get a glimpse of our native land in what we are accustomed to call its prehistoric times, that the whole narrative has a double interest for Scotsmen.

As an undoubted historic landmark we may take the reign of King Tuathal Techtmar, already referred to, which is critically fixed as having closed about 160 A.D., though some writers give a slightly earlier date. He was the ancestor of our present King Edward VII., as the latter can with certainty trace his genealogy back to King Earc of Irish Dalriada in Ulster, father of Loarne and Fergus, the first kings of Scottish

Dalriada, who came to Argyle (Airer Gaidhel = The District or Country of the Gael) in 498 A.D., and whose ancestors are recorded in the Irish annals for centuries further back, all of the royal Scotic blood of Ireland.

Tuathal had a long reign and left a deep mark in Erinn, but prior to his ascension there had been an interregnum of twenty-five years through rebellion of the Servile Tribes of Ireland (the Attach Tuatha). Prior to this interregnum several Scotic kings, ancestors of King Tuathal, had reigned, though it is uncertain if their race penetrated to Ulster until a century later, and this point makes it questionable whether the Uisneachs were, as Professor O'Curry believes, of the Irian branch of the Milesian or Scotic race, or, as Mr William F. Skene asserts, of the Cruithne or Celto-Pictish race, though Skene's curious and uncritical antipathy to the Dalriadic Scots may have misled him. In any case, whether Scotic or Pictish, the Uisneachs were pure Celtic in blood, as was also King Conchubhar or Conor, the ruler of Uladh or Ulster, in whose reign they lived and died. King Conor lived in pagan times, and died in the year 33 A.D.

The possible truth of the tale is enhanced by its

simplicity, the probability of its incidents, the absence of miracles, exaggerations, and those other absurdities which mark tales of the same period and the ballads of later days; and, above all, its probability is almost certified by the numerous place-names which its characters have left in Scotland and Ireland, and which have stood unchanged for ages. These are referred to later, and as evidence of the story a quotation from one of the most learned authorities on Celtic literature may be useful. Dr Eugène O'Curry, Professor of History and Archæology in the Catholic University of Ireland, speaking of the three tales, describes the second and third (those of Lir and Tuireann) as "pure romances," but of the "Sons of Uisneach," he says it is referred to the Milesian (or Scotic) time and race, and is, though somewhat "poetised, founded on true history with real historical characters." Elsewhere he writes, "There is no reason to doubt this story is a true one. Almost all the characters introduced into it are so well known in Gaedhelic history that to doubt the authenticity of its leading facts would be to throw doubt on the truthfulness of all our most prized chronicles and historical documents."

The story of the Uisneachs is recorded in part or

in whole in three ancient MSS., not to mention other accounts of later date.

The oldest is that in the Book of Leinster, a vellum MS. compiled about 1150 A.D. by Finn Mac Gorman, Bishop of Kildare, and preserved in Trinity College, Dublin. The portion in which the story of the Uisneachs appears is under a general head of Historic Tales, to be told to Kings and Chiefs, "Seven times fifty Stories, *i.e.* five times fifty Prime Stories, twice fifty Secondary Stories . . . and these are the Prime Stories:— Destructions and Preyings and Courtships and Battles and Caves and Navigations and Tragedies and Expeditions and Elopements and Conflagrations." In this section occurs the tract under "Elopement" (Aithidhé), entitled "Athed Dheirdri re Macaibh Uisnigh," *i.e.* "Elopement of Deirdre with the Sons of Uisneach." This narrative gives many details not found in the later Irish MS., and is preferred by O'Curry as the most reliable, as it is the most ancient version of the story.

The second in date is preserved in Advocates' Library, Edinburgh, forming part of the Glenmasan MS., and bears date 1238 A.D.[1] It is written, like

---

[1] See Preface for reference to Professor Mackinnon's recent translation of this MS., and his remarks as to the date of this copy.

other old Celtic MSS., in the Irish characters, and in the language then and still common to Ireland and the Celts of Scotland. It happily supplies what the two Irish versions omit, DEIRDRE'S LAMENT ON LEAVING ALBAN (or Scotland), in which she graphically refers to the numerous places in the county of Argyle which she and her friends had visited in their wanderings.

The third version is one contained in a vellum MS. preserved in the Library of the Trinity College, Dublin, compiled, in the year 1391 A.D., by Gilla-Isa Mór Mac Firbisigh, one of the hereditary historians of Lecain Mac Firbisigh, county Sligo, and written in the MS. work known as "The Yellow Book of Lecain" (Leabhar Buidhe Lecan).

In criticising the latter version, Professor O'Curry finds in it evidence of some modification of the original story; but he finds that, following the usual course of such changes, the ancient more condensed narratives tend to become amplified or more storified as centuries pass. On the other hand (as in the story of the Uisneachs, where several versions of the same tale exist, each covering circumstances occurring at different times or places) the later amplification may be the result of some later editor's endeavour to embody all information available from various sources, just as in the present work an endeavour has been made to collect information on the subject from the various accounts and collate them into one narrative.

Professor O'Curry admits that certain additions are obviously anachronisms of a later date, as for example where a Norseman is brought in to slay the sons of Uisneach (in one of the versions), no Norsemen appearing in Ireland until centuries later, unless the Fomorian pirates were of that race; the reason for the error being that some late editor, wishing to remove from the kindly Celts the disgrace of the murder, transferred a Norseman from the eighth century to the first, and cut off three heads at one blow with Manannan Mac Lir's sword!

So similar, however, are these more amplified versions in the main body of the narrative that O'Curry admits that the most learned and critical eye is puzzled to tell whether they may not really have formed the true original story, and the condensations be only a more modern epitome, the greater number of modern features appearing in the amplified versions being possibly due to the fact that the more detailed narrative was the most popular for reading and transcription.

CHAPTER IV

The Uisneachs' Birth and Education—Skye—Conor Macnessa—Birth of Deirdre—Caffa the Druid—Deirdre's Wooing—Flight to Scotland.

THE brightest hour of Ulster's early history, partly mythical or legendary, was that of the champions of the Red or Royal Branch at Emania, the capital of Ulster in the days of King Fergus and Conor Macnessa shortly before the Christian era began.

At that time Caffa (Cathbhad), a druid of the Irinian Celts of Ulster, had three daughters. Dectum, the eldest, became mother of the famous Cuchulain. Albe, the second, was the mother of the three sons of Uisneach, Naisi, Ainlé, and Ardan (or Dardan). The third daughter, Finncaemh, was mother of a famous champion, Conall Cearnagh, whose name still survives in Dunchonill, one of the Garveloch Isles south of Oban.

The present writer has been unable to get any satisfactory evidence as to the father of Naisi and his two brothers. A fragment of a tract on the Clan Rudhraighe, or the ancient Irinian royal race of

Uladh (Ulster) gives Rudhraighe (Red Prince) as the common ancestor, whose son Congall Claringnech had two sons, Caffa (Cathbhad) the Druid and Uislenn, the latter of whom is there said to be the father of the three sons of Uisneach. But this contradicts the earlier statement that Caffa was grandfather of the Uisneachs, not their uncle. In several places in the "Yellow Book of Lecain" they are called sons of Uisle, which resembles the Uislenn of the above fragment. If Uisle or Uislenn was not a son of Caffa (or son-in-law, and so husband to Albe, the mother of the heroes), it may be supposed that these names are merely two more of the very many ways in which the name of Uisneach is written.

It is indicative of the familiar intercourse in these early times between Ireland and the West of Alban, that these five champions were educated at a kind of military school at Sgathaig in the Island of Skye. This spot can still be identified on a projecting rock on the west side of Sleat, near the mouth of Loch Eishort, where exist the remains of an ancient castle called Dunscath. A little way out into the loch lies a tiny islet on which stands a vitrified fort, also called Dunsgathaig or Dunscath, probably the supposed school of the Amazonian lady champion

Scathaidh[1] and her fair daughter Aife, with whom Cuchulain fell in love! Alban evidently stood high at this time as a military training ground, for Cuchulain was counselled to go either to Scathaidh or to another Alban teacher Domhnall (Donnal), and schools of poetry and literature seem to have also existed there. Cuchulain's travels and adventures in Scotland are full of natural incidents and curious allusions to the customs of that early period, and throw light on the meanings of many place-names which still survive.

Mr Skene points out as illustrative of the great age of these vitrified forts and also of the Uisneach story that no personal names (apart from mere legend) can historically be associated with any of them except with the three forts which are connected with the Uisneachs, viz., Dunsgathaig, Dun Mac Uisneach at Ledaig, and Dun Deardhui-l, near Inverness, referred to later.

The heights of Dunsgathaig command a glorious view of the Cuillin Hills of Skye (not the Cu-chullin

---

[1] O'Curry's MS. Materials. Skene apparently omits to note Scathaidh's gender, to whom he refers as the father of Aife ("Celtic Scot.," vol. iii. p. 128). In the Cuchulain Saga, Aife is said to be an Amazonian rival of Scathaidh, conquered by Cuchulain.

Hills, as some writers call them). Deirdre at a later day called the three brothers, "The Three Falcons of Sliabh Cuillinn;"[1] but while Skene claims this honour for the Skye hills, Dr Joyce claims it for the isolated hill in the south of county Armagh now called Slieve Gullion, "The Hill of the Holly Trees"—celebrated in Irish song and story.

It is related of Cuchulain's return to Ireland that he passed *Ceann Tiree* (Land's Head), now better known as Cantyre, which has therefore kept its name unchanged for nineteen centuries! On the return of the heroes to their native land they found that King Fergus had resigned his throne for the fair face of Nessa, a lovely but scheming Irish dame who had stipulated by an antenuptial contract of marriage that Conchubhar or Conor, her son by a previous husband (Fachtna the Wise), should hold the royal power for one year. For this she carefully educated her son; and the young prince, ever after called Conor Macnessa, thus strangely raised to a throne, so ingratiated himself to the senators of Ulster by his wisdom, to its warriors by his courage, and to its women by his beauty, that at the close of his year's probation they refused to follow King Fergus Mac

[1] Pronounce Sleeve Coolin.

Roigh and defiantly chose Conor as their chief, declining to be ruled by a man who had sold his kingdom for one woman, and might do so again for another. King Conor grew in favour and beauty, and the unlucky Fergus was compelled, after some fighting, to smother his wrath and accept the compensations of his beautiful wife.

Some years later amid certain dire portents, too physiologically described in the tale for transcription, there was born a most lovely little maid, the daughter of Felimid (Feidlimidh), the court historian or secretary, and in respect that the Druid Caffa (Cathbhad), grandfather of Cuchulain and the sons of Uisneach, foretold terrible evil to the people of Ulster through her, she was named DEIRDRIU or DEIRDRE.

Professor O'Curry says the meaning of this name is quite uncertain, and Dr Joyce can only add it "is said to mean alarm."

The prophetic description of the young lady by the Druid is peculiarly Celtic in its form : " A maiden, fair, tall, long haired, for whom champions will contend, whom many high kings will solicit—kings who shall [undergo the toils of war in King Conor's pay for her sake]. Her lips will be cherry red and her teeth as the pearl, wherefore shall mighty kings be envious of her lovely, faultless form." So far the text of the MS. has been in prose, but there follow here six verses of more ancient poetry addressed to the child by the Druid, referring to the misfortunes likely to come on Ulster, its warriors, and herself through her wonderful beauty. All this, of course, would be written after the event, and the description was probably made from tradition of Deirdre in her prime of womanhood. While the earliest MS. of the tale is of 1150 A.D. (less than a century after the Norman Conquest), Professor O'Curry believes the existence of the story can be traced back to 600 A.D. The poetry may thus be over twelve centuries old; and if, as is generally supposed, the prose portions represent parts, the poetry of which had been lost before being committed to writing, these verses may be looked on with the reverence due to extreme antiquity.

The six verses, as translated by O'Curry in *Atlantis Magazine*, are as follows :—

"O! Deirdriu, for whom we have prophesied,
When thou art a comely-faced famous woman,
The Ultonians shall suffer in thy time,
Thou daughter fair of Feidhlimidh ;[1]

" They shall be jealous even afterwards
On thy account, oh blushing maiden !

---

[1] Pronounced Felimid.

It is in thy time shall be, hear thou this,
The exile of the sons of Uislé.

"It is in thy time a wicked deed
Shall be hereafter perpetrated in Emhain
Its wickedness shall be rued, even afterwards
When shall fall the sons of mighty kings.[1]

"It is through thee, thou gifted maiden,
 [Shall happen] the exile of Ferghus from Ulster,
And a deed from which cryings shall come forth,
The killing of Fiacha, the son of Conchobhar.[2]

"It is through thy fault, thou gifted maiden,
 [Shall come] the killing of Gerc, the son of Illadan,
And a deed of not smaller penalty,
The killing of Eoghan (Owen), the son of Durrthacht.[3]

"An ugly, fierce deed thou wilt commit [4]
On account of the anger of the high king of Ulster.
Thy grave shall lie in a place not native;
Thy history shall be illustrious, oh Deirdriu."

On hearing such evil bodings, the assembled warriors said, "Let her be killed"; but King Conor humanely said, "No! she shall be nursed, and I myself shall marry her when she is grown." So she was reared in an enclosed and separate *lis*,[5] hidden from

[1] The massacre of the Uisneach clan.
[2] See page 64, death of Fiacha.
[3] See page 71, death of Eoghan Mac Durrthacht.
[4] Her own death.
[5] An earthen enclosure; probably round a separate house in this case.

and seeing no man, guarded by her nurse, her tutor, and visited only by a woman named Lavarcam (Leabharcham), a female satirist or court singer (*chainte*). The court satirists of Old Ireland had even greater privileges than the court fools of later days, and could go anywhere, and say anything.

Thus the years of Deirdre's childhood fled, and she came forth in her beauty to see and be seen by the sons of Ulster. "Gossiping Lavarcam" had evidently filled her head with some nonsense, and seems to have led her to place no trust on the king's promise of marriage. One day her tutor shed the blood of a calf upon the snow, and a raven hopped up, pecking at the crimson mark. The contrast of colours touched Deirdre's imagination. "These are the colours," she cried, "my beloved must have—his hair like the raven, his cheeks like the blood, and his skin like the snow." "Dignity and choice to thee!" wished Irish Lavarcam. "He is not far from thee . . . Naisi, the son of Uisneach." "I shall not be well," said Deirdre, "until I have seen him." "Love laughs at locksmiths," and so did Lavarcam. Regardless of the king's command she wiled Naisi, unknown to Deirdre, to chant on the mound in the centre of the Rath, or green, at Emania, where Deirdre might view him without being seen, he all unconscious of the beauty who was watching him. Language fails the annalist to praise sufficiently the sweetness of Naisi's voice in song, and one verse in a later part of the story depicts some chorus singing by Naisi and his two brothers as they returned from the hunting in Alban to their huts, where Deirdre awaited them. Their three voices are described by three Irish words representing respectively, the bass strings of the ancient harp for Naisi's voice, the tenor, or intermediate strings, for Ardan's voice, and the sweet upper strings for the higher notes of Ainlé.

Returning to that scene at the Rath of Emania, Deirdre stole out towards Naisi as if to pass him. Though he did not know her, custom in Ireland permitted him to speak to *himself* in admiration of the lovely vision!

"Beautiful is (she) who passes by" is the nearest approach permissible to what Naisi said, and a curious conversation followed between the two, revealing much of the peculiar liberty, and even power, which women then had in Ireland, exceeding anything enjoyed by them in the later days of so-called chivalry. To the modern reader, it sounds like a Leap-year wooing, and poor Deirdre seems to have set her cap at Naisi, though probably she had no other covering on her beautiful head than her golden hair.

Naisi fell a victim at once, for no sooner had she gone than "he raised his chant out of him," as the chronicler says, *i.e.* he sang aloud in evident triumph. His brothers, hearing the sound, came to him, and on learning what he told them, sought to divert his thoughts from Deirdre, but in vain. He related to them how she had touched him and what she had said, and they at once admitted, "Evil will be of it, yet though there be, thou shalt not be under disgrace as long as we shall be alive. We will go with her to another country. There is not in Erinn a king who will not bid us welcome."

Deirdre's boldness, though strange to modern ideas, was evidently in accordance with some well-accepted custom by which a man could not, without shame to himself, refuse a woman if she plainly indicated her love for him.

From the narrative, they evidently decided quickly to face the call of fate, and that night they fled, taking Deirdre with them, also many of their companions in arms, their attendants, and their women— some four hundred and fifty-four persons in all.

For some time they evaded the pursuit of Conor

by going westward to Ballyshannon (Eas Ruaidh), in Donegal, then south-westward and eastward to the Hill of Howth (Ben Edair) at Dublin Bay. Then on to Rathlin Island, whence they were compelled to sail for Scotland, or Alban, where the Irish chronicler leaves them "sheltering in a desert there."

CHAPTER V

Loch Etive—Deirdre's First Home—Dun Mac Uisneach—Remains of the Fort—Clach Manessa—Eilean Uisneachan—Deirdre's Drawing-room—Her Children—Adventures at Inverness—Dunadd and Duntroon Castle—Scottish Scenery—Recalled to Ireland—"Deirdre's Lament."

THE Irish MSS. give so brief notice of the wanderers' life in Scotland that they have to be combined with the MS. in the Advocates' Library, or with the notice in the Dean of Lismore's Book, both containing "Deirdre's Lament." These, with the names of the places visited by the exiles, enable us to follow their wanderings in Scotland. Their first shelter in Alban was probably Loch Etive; and another proof of the great age of the story may be noted in the fact that the name "Scot," or "Scotland," is not once mentioned, nor is there any reference even to the Dalriadic kingdom, for they visited the Alban coasts centuries before the Dalriads crossed the seas. Up to the tenth century Scotland was known as Alban, and the war-cry of the Celtic men of Galloway at the Battle of the Standard in 1138 was still "Albanach! Albanach!"

A very beautiful verse in "Deirdre's Lament" speaks of Loch Etive and its glen as her first home:—

> "Glen Etive, oh Glen Etive,
> There was raised *my earliest* home;
> Beautiful were its woods in the dawning,
> When the sun (light) fell on Glen Etive."

Their fleet must have passed through the sound now called Kererra, and rounding Dunolly Point, crossed to Ardnamuich Bay—to which the Norse of later days unnecessarily added the Ness—making it, as now, Ard-na-muichnish Point and Bay.

At the head of the bay lies the little hillock, or dun, erroneously called Beregonium, which is still called by the Celtic population Dun Mac Sniochan, a corruption of Dun Mhic Uisneach. On the top may be traced the ancient vitrified fort which the exiles inhabited, but probably did not build, as such forts are uncommon in Ireland. This may have been the headquarters of the small tribe which accompanied them, for it is unlikely that all the four hundred and fifty people travelled about on the various hunting expeditions.

Of the age of these vitrified forts no certain word can be said. From metallic remains found in them, they seem to have been used during the bronze and early iron period, but this is no certain proof of the date of their erection.

In Dun Mhic Uisneach few discoveries were made in an exploration conducted some years ago; a worn iron brooch of circular form, a piece of enamelled bronze, and a much decayed fragment of an iron sword were, apart from the bones of animals, all that could be found. The fort is chiefly on the southern end of the hill, and many of its outer walls, as well as the foundation lines of one of the dwelling-houses, with four apartments, were uncovered, though now hid by the grass. Most of the outer walls have fallen down the steep sides of the dun, though the foundations, of considerable strength, can be traced in various places. There is a shallow well, and one of the two grassy slopes leading down to the meadow on the east is called "Bealach na Bhan Righ" (The Way of the King's Wife or Queen). A neighbouring bay is Cambus Nāish, a possible corruption of the name of the leader, Naisi, whose name appears in as many different forms as do those of "Uisneach" and of "Deirdre." The Duke of Argyll points out that dried seaweed was used as fuel in vitrifying these masses of stone, being built into the wall like lime, and afterwards heaped round the building and fired, when the potash in the seaweed acted as a natural solvent of the silica in the stone, and fused it into a solid wall. Microscopic scraps of unburnt seaweed were found amid the stones when broken up, and thus led to the above supposition. A good plan, and much information as to the dun, will be found in Dr Angus Smith's book, "Loch Etive and the Sons of Uisneach."

The wanderers did not constantly reside at Benderloch, but had some hunting lodges, or huts, further up Loch Etive, and in Glen Etive.

The mouth of Loch Etive, at the Falls of Lora, is only two miles from Dun Mac Uisneach, and the exiles must have rowed or sailed up past the spot where now stands, on the shore near Taynuilt, the huge boulder stone called Clach Manessa, or The Stone of Manessa. As the name "Manessa" is unknown, apart from its similarity to Mac Nessa, it has been suggested this may be a monument to King Conor, who was always called Mac Nessa after his mother; while Dr Angus Smith mentions that others rail at this doctrine, and ask if the "Ma" may not be a corruption of the Welsh, "moen," a stone, and the boulder be thus a memorial to Nessa herself, the "Clach," Alban-Celtic for "stone," being added by a later age ignorant of the Welsh-Celtic "moen," just as the Norse added "Nish" or "Ness" to the name of Ard-na-Muich, making it Ard-na-muichnish. The latter name has been further maltreated by the addition of the English "Point," when Ard, Ness, and Point all have the same meaning, though the name, as it now stands, is valuable as proving the three nations which have marked it with their language.

Proceeding up Loch Etive towards the twin peaks of Cruachan (also an Irish name, see page 77), close to Taynuilt, on the rising ground south of the loch, lies the ancient wood still called Coille Nāish (The Wood of Naisi), with Ben or Cruach Ardain to the south (spelled Ard-dhuine on the O.S. maps), and a mile south of Taynuilt is the farm of Ardainaidh (Airdeny on the O.S. maps). Associated with a rock on the north side, beyond Bonawe quarries, at the point called Ruadh nan Draighnean (The Point of the Blackthorn), there are traditions of the daughter of a king of Ulster who eloped with a legendary Earl of Ardchattan, evidently some distorted tradition of the real story.

At Bonawe and Taynuilt the River Awe flows into the loch, and the latter turns suddenly northwards along the base of Cruachan, on the slopes of which traces of Deirdre's and the Uisneach's names are found. A few miles up the loch's western shore lies the Bay of Cadderly, off the north point of which is a small rocky islet called Eilean Uisneachan—the island of the Uisneachs. It is only 30 or 40 yards in its longest line, but amid its bushes lie the remains of some ancient ruined dwelling-places, possibly fragments of the hunting lodge which sheltered the exiles; and, on the adjoining shore, tradition tells of the wonderful apple orchards of the Uisneachs, long since swept away.

At the head of the loch the River Etive comes down through the glen, and as the valley ascends the scenery becomes grander and more solemn in its rocky desolation. A few miles north of Kinloch Etive there juts out into the right side of the glen a vast rock, standing black pointed and fierce against the sky. On the O.S. maps it is called Ben Kettelin (or Cetlin). It has another name, however, *Grianan Dartheil* or Deardhuil, the Boudoir or Sunny Room of Darthula, three of the many Alban forms of Deirdre's name, while in the valley below is Ach-an-Dartheil = The Field of Deirdre. Macpherson uses the name

Darthula in his "Poems of Ossian," but the tale there is scarcely recognisable, though not without beauty.

The Ultonian Chronicle tells of the exiles seeking refuge "in a desert in Alban," and no language could more graphically describe this wilderness of Glen Etive. It was at the head of this glen that Robert Louis Stevenson, in "Kidnapped," left Alan Breck and David Balfour for some days, safe from pursuit in the wilds of Corrynakeigh.

How long the Uisneachs hunted round Loch Etive, or the length of their sojourn in Scotland, we know not, but two children were born to Naisi and Deirdre while they were in Alban. Gaiar, a son, famous in later days, and who, after defeating King Conor Mac Nessa, divided the throne with him for a year, but subsequently abdicated, preferring to live quietly with his friend, and his father's friend, Manannan Mac Lir in the Island of Emhain (Aven) of the apple trees, now identified with the Island of Arran. The other child was a daughter, to whom was given the name Aebgreine (pronounced Aev-grein), *i.e.* "Like the Sun."

By-and-bye trouble arose with the Uisneachs. Notwithstanding their 150 hounds, they were unable to supply the needs of four hundred and fifty mouths by hunting, and it is said they laid their hands on the cattle of the country people, who rose in arms. Another account, not inconsistent with the above, tells how they were invited to lend their military services to the king of the Picts at Inverness, and that they went thither, evidently travelling up the Great Glen, past Loch Lochy and Loch Ness towards the eastern side. At Inverness an incident occurred resembling the experiences in Egypt of Abraham and Sarah. The chronicle, as translated by O'Curry, says, " They set up their houses at night. It was on account of the woman that the houses were so made that none should see her with them, that they should not be killed on her account. At a certain time now the steward [of the Pictish king] went at early dawn, making a turn round the house, where he saw the couple asleep.

"He went then and awakened the king. 'We have not found,' said he, 'a wife worthy of thee till this day. There is with Naisi, the son of Uisneach, a woman worthy of the kings of the western world. Let Naisi be killed, *immediately*, and let the woman wed with thee.' 'Not so,' said the king, 'but go thou and ask her secretly.' The steward performed what he was desired towards her before night. *She told her husband that night at once."* Then the chronicle adds, "When no good could be got of her, the sons of Uisneach were ordered to go into dangers, battles, and difficulties, for the purpose that they should be killed." Out of all these dangers their valour and skill delivered them, but when another conspiracy as to Deirdre came to their knowledge, they left suddenly at night for the south, and were allowed to go unmolested.

As already mentioned, our heroine's name is still remembered in the valley of the Ness in a vitrified fort called Dun Deardhuil, or Cnoc Dheardhuil; and Mr Skene thinks there is also a remarkable identification with the three brothers in a paragraph in Adamnan's "Life of St Columba," where, writing of the saint's journey to Inverness, his biographer mentions three localities in the Great Glen in which the names of the Uisneachs are contained and may be commemorated—the mount or district of Cainle, Arc-Ardan and *flumen Nesae*, the last the River Ness itself! These place-names, thus proved to exist in the sixth or seventh centuries, give some evidence of the presence of the Uisneachs in that region in very early times, and tell of the dignity attaching to their persons. The river Ness, Loch Ness and Inverness town may thus be named after the chief of the band.

At one period of their life in Scotland, the military qualities of the exiles led to their visiting a region famous two centuries later as the first territory held by the Dalriadic Scots (probably under Cairpre Riata) in Alban, Dunmonadh or Dunadd, from which they are called " The Three Dragons of Dunmonadh." This dun has been identified with Dunadd, sometimes Dunatt, a hill 150 feet in height, in Crinan Moss, on the bank of the River Add (or Airdh), just where the Crinan Canal emerges on the waters of Loch Crinan.

On the opposite side of the valley, and nearer the sea, stands Duntroon Castle, whereby hangs a tale; for Naisi, on one occasion of his returning from Inverness, forgot his faithful Deirdre and carried a gift to some fair daughter of the Lord of Duntroon, on hearing which his wife—but here are her own words, preserved in her Lament :—

> " Upon my hearing of this
> My head was filled with jealousy ;
> I put my little boat on the water,
> Indifferent to me was life or death ;
>
> " They pursued me on the float,
> Ainli and Ardan, who uttered not falsehood,

>They turned me inwards,
>Two that would subdue in battle a hundred."
>*Skene's translation in Dean of Lismore's Book.*

Deirdre always speaks with sincere affection of these her two brothers-in-law, but in the present instance the praise of them is an evident reflection on her naughty husband, whom here she does not praise. A happy reconciliation followed, for she adds, "For Naisi gave his word in truth."

Though Dun Mac Uisneach was probably the tribal headquarters, Naisi and his family moved over various parts of the district now known as Argyleshire, of which he had some kind of chieftainship. "Deirdre's Lament" names several of these places, and her references clearly indicate a personal knowledge of them. Some verses are inserted later from this poem, where she mentions, amongst other places, Loch Swin and its dun, near Crinan on the Sound of Jura; Innis-draighende, now Innistrynich on Loch Awe; Coillchuan, which recalls Kilchurn at the head of Loch Awe, whose mediæval castle still adorns the rocky knoll amid the meadows of the Orchy, where Deirdre and her brothers dwelt; Glen Laidhe, which Skene connects with Glen Lochy, where there is a Ben Laidhe; Glen Masan, at the top of Holy Loch in Cowal; Glendaruadh is Glen-daruel at the top of Loch Ridden, one of the arms of the Kyles of Bute where the red funnelled *Columba* now ploughs the waters once stirred by Naisi's galley; Glen Urchain is Glen Orchy, near Dalmally ; and Glen Eitche is Glen Etive, Deirdre's first home.

In these ancient Celtic poems the modern reader is impressed with the constant sense of Nature's beauties expressed in them, peculiar at that early time and among a people on the fringe of civilisation. The poetic feeling manifested by these children of the moor and mountain is in striking contrast with the antipathies of later ages down to the eighteenth century, when even a Goldsmith could not admire the "fine prospects" of Scotland because so many were spoiled "by hills," or a Gibbon had no language but that of contempt for the "gloomy heaths" of Caledonia. It is pleasant to dwell on these faraway times, before international antipathies obscured men's vision to the "beautiful" in a land outside their own. One Irish writer of the twelfth century, quoted by O'Curry and Sullivan, says :—

"Beloved to me are the beautiful woods of Alban."

Then, like a true son of Erinn, he adds :—

"Though strange, I love dearer still
This tree from the woods of Erinn."

A line in Columba's song on the outlook from Iona shows that he too possessed the seeing eye for nature.

"The thunder of the crowding seas upon the shore"

is a glorious sounding picture of the western ocean which then, as now, beat on that lonely shore.

Viewing "Deirdre's Lament" merely as literature, and apart from its historic value, it is the earliest word on the beauties of our native land which any language has recorded.

Meantime events had been occurring in Ireland which were to terminate with alarming suddenness these happy days in Alban. News of the exiles had not failed to reach King Conor Macnessa. One narrative credits Fergus, the ex-king, with proposing to recall Naisi and his band, that their services as warriors might be recovered for their native land. To this proposal Conor rather grudgingly agreed on condition that the Uisneachs should make their submission to him on their return.

A more detailed narrative, not inconsistent with the other, represents Conor as having given a magnificent feast in a new palace he had built. In the presence of his flattering guests he asks, "Was ever a palace seen so fair as this of mine?" and dissatisfied with their shouts of "Never," he bade them guess what it lacked. When all were silent, he said it needed the presence of these three "renowned and exalted youths, these three sun risings of the valour of the Gael, the three noble sons of Uisneach." Then those present gladly agreed that the three brothers should be sent for, as they had conquered a large part of Alban, and might be altogether lost to Erinn if not invited to return immediately.

The wily Conor, however, planned to have his foes unconditionally in his power, but Cuchulain and Conall Cearnagh, to whom he first offered the embassy, fiercely refused to go without a clear pledge of safe-conduct for the Uisneachs. The jealous king avoided giving such a pledge, and with a cloud of words beguiled his step-father Fergus to sail to Alban and bring back the exiles. The good-natured, but stupid, Fergus joyfully departed with his two sons, Illan the Fair and Buiné the Red.

Both narratives agree that Fergus found his countrymen at Loch Etive (variously named Loch Eitche or Loch n' Eite), in Alban, and at the Dainghion Mhic n' Uisneach, the fortress of the sons of Uisneach. If this was the dun at the head of Ardnamuich Bay, there is still distinctly visible the little gravelled cove, which might serve as a harbour, surrounded by rocks on each side for some distance. Deirdre and her husband were playing chess when they heard the shout of Fergus as his boat entered the harbour. The distance from the harbour to the top of the dun is quite consistent with Naisi's recognition of accent in the voice, though too far to distinguish words. Evidently even at that early date the Irish Celt had an accent different from that of Alban.

"That is the voice of a man of Erinn," he said. Deirdre, in terror, had also recognised the voice, but hiding her thoughts, said, "No! it was the voice of a man of Alban." Again Fergus shouted, and again Naisi said, "This *is* the call of an Erinn man," and a second time Deirdre refused to have it so, until a third call from Fergus brought Ardan to the edge of the cliff to look down on the shore and recognise King Fergus.

As Ardan went down to greet his friend, Deirdre acknowledged to Naisi that she had, at the first, known Fergus' voice. "Why didst thou then conceal it, my queen," said Naisi; and Deirdre answered, "Because I saw in a dream last night three birds come from Emania of Macha, carrying three sups of honey in their beaks. The honey they left with us, but took away three sups of our blood." "What, then, do you draw from this?" asked Naisi. She replied, "That Fergus comes with words of peace from Conor; for honey is not more sweet than the peace messages of a treacherous man."

Meantime Ardan had met and kissed Fergus and his sons, and was asking for the tidings from Erinn. The party climbed the dun and met Naisi and his wife, who also kissed them, asking also for news from beloved Ireland. Fergus, in all good faith, cheerfully told them of Conor's message and their recall to their beloved Erinn. Before Naisi could reply, Deirdre's quick wit and fears broke in. "It is not meet," she said, "for them to go thither, for greater is their sway in Alban than the rule of Conor in Ireland."

"Ah," said Fergus, "the land of one's birth is better than all things. It is a cheerless thing to the richest and greatest not to see his own country every day."

"True," said Naisi, "and Erinn is dearer to me than Alban, even if I have more here."

Deirdre still urged her fears and bitterly opposed leaving the happy home in Alban, but her pleadings were in vain. "We will go to Erinn," said Naisi, and they went.

It was while on the waters, as she gazed at the receding hills of Alban, that Deirdre is said to have uttered the Lament which bears her name. "My love to thee, beloved land of the east; sad am I to leave thy bays and lochs, thy meadows and thy green hills."

Many of these historic tales, as they have now come down to us, are partly in prose, but it is recognised that such portions represent only those parts of the original poem of which the poetic form has been lost, as the oldest versions contain most poetry and least prose. Dr Geoffrey Keating (quoted by O'Curry), in his preface to his History of Ireland, says that history in ancient times was all in verse, for its better remembrance and preservation before the art of writing was introduced. As ages passed and history was reduced to writing, memory failed to record the metre in full, and the transcribers had to supply the poetic blanks in prose, from oral tradition.

The following verses are adapted from Skene's translation of the "Lament," which appeared in his introduction to the Dean of Lismore's Book. A literal translation, like Skene's, is invaluable, just as the skeleton is to the young anatomist, but the ordinary reader is so apt to sigh for some flesh and blood, that the present writer has ventured to take some liberties with Mr Skene's text for the sake of a more harmonious reading.

"DEIRDRE'S LAMENT

"Belovèd land, dear eastern land,
   Alban with its wonders,;
Oh, that I ne'er depart from thee,
   But that I go from thee with Naisi.

"Belov'd Dun-Fidgha and Dun-Finn,
   And dear the hill above them;
Belov'd is Innis-draighen too,[1]
   And dear to me Dun Suibhne.[2]

"Coil-chuan too, [Coilchuan [3]]
   Where Ainlé would, alas, resort.
Too short, too short were these glad days
   With Naisi in the lands of Alban.

"Glenlaidhe, [Glenlaidhe [4]]
   I slept beneath thy soothing shelter.
Fish and deer, and badger too
   My daily feast were in Glenlaidhe.

---

[1] Innistrynich, Loch Awe.

[2] Pronounced "Sweeny." Probably Dunrostan, the hill overlooking the mouth of Loch Swin, where Castle Sweeny stands. South of Crinan, Argyleshire.

[3] Kilchurn, Loch Awe.

[4] Possibly Glen Lochy, where there is a Ben Laidhe.

"Glen-Masan, [O Glen Masan![1]]
High were its herbs, and white their blossoms,
And sweetly lone our resting-place
On the green, green grass of Invermasan.

"Glen Etive, [O Glen Etive!]
In thee was raised my earliest home.
Beautiful its woods at the dawning,
When the sun rose on Glen Etive.

"Glen Urchain, [O Glen Urchain![2]]
The far-seen glen of gentle slopes;
No man more happy was, and joyful,
Than Naisi was in thee, Glen Urchain!

"Glen Daruel, [O Glen Daruel!]
My love to every dweller in thee;
The cuckoo's voice on bending bough
Sweet sounds upon thy bens, Glen Daruel!

"Belovèd Draighen and its wave-beat shore,
Belov'd its waters and its pure white sand.
Oh, to depart not from thee, Alban,
But that I go with my beloved."

Of all the twice ten thousand lines which the poetic fancy of ages has penned on Scotland's hills and dales, her mountain bens and trotting "burns," her hawthorn blossom and her blooming heather, the

[1] At head of Holy Loch, Argyleshire.
[2] Probably Glen Orchy, whose long vista of beauty is enhanced by the smoothness of its lateral curves.

reader may remember that these lines of Deirdre are probably the most ancient now in existence. With them we forget the nineteen centuries which separate her day from ours, and seem to hear her voice in the woods of Invermasan, under the shadow of Ben More.[1] It was natural that she should love Scotland, and the verses really afford another proof of the verity of the tale. They are the expressions of one who had known no joy or peace in her native land of Ireland, where her childhood was a dreary seclusion and her brief public life a daily terror of flight from a hated enemy. In Alban alone she had tasted the sweetness of life. There her children had been born, and there had passed the too brief years of her happy married life. Now all was changed with a suddenness prophetic of evil, and with a sad heart she watched the distant hills of Alban as hour after hour they sank on the horizon and ever nearer arose the land where dwelt her enemy.

[1] At Invermasan the River Masan joins the Echaig two miles below Loch Eck and about five miles from Sandbank, or Ardnadam Pier, on the Firth of Clyde.

CHAPTER VI

Landing in Ireland—The Traitor Borach—Arrival at Emania—Siege of the Red Branch House—The Sortie, Surrender, and Massacre of the Uisneachs—Deirdre a Captive—Eoghan Mac Durrthacht—Deirdre's Death.

ACCORDING to Irish tradition, the returning exiles and Fergus landed in Ireland at Ballycastle, opposite Rathlin Island, where a rock on the shore is still called "Carraig Uisneach" (The Rock or Craig of Uisneach).

On the very beach they were met by a traitor. It had been intended that King Fergus should accompany them to King Conor's house at Emania, but Conor had resolved otherwise. One of his ruffians, Borach, met Fergus with a mysterious invitation to an ale banquet—they had no potheen in Ireland then.

The Uisneachs could not accept this, as they had vowed to break bread in Ireland first at Conor's table. Fergus and Deirdre both feared treachery, and dreaded this banquet, for, according to Irish custom, it would be a mortal affront to refuse, and it might go on for days, thus depriving the Uisneachs of Fergus' protection. Conor and Borach had foreseen this. Fergus very reluctantly confided his trust to his two sons and went to the banquet. "Selling his honour for ale," said Deirdre sadly. She now entreated her husband to return to Rathlin Island until Fergus was free to go with them to the king, but Naisi's angry pride and the confidence of Fergus' sons led them to Emania. Throughout the journey, again and again Deirdre expressed her forebodings of evil and her fears and compassion for the "beautiful sons of Uisneach." She had no selfish complainings; all her expressions are for her husband's and her brothers' danger. Her anxieties by day brought dreams of woe at night, but to none of these would Naisi listen. When they reached Drum-Sailech,[1] the ridge where Armagh now stands, and saw the Rath of Emania in the distance, Deirdre's fears broke out afresh, and for the last time she entreated Naisi to turn aside to Dundalgan (now Dundalk), there to abide with the mighty Cuchulain until Fergus returned. But again

---

[1] Drum-Sailech, the ridge of the willows. "Sailech," whence Scottish "Saugh." "Siller saughs wi' downy buds."—TANNAHILL.

her husband's pride pushed him on to his fate, as he sadly replied, "This we cannot do, my beloved! for it might show we had fear, and we have none!"

Their reception was startlingly unfriendly. They were not admitted to the palace, but ordered to reside in the House of the Red or Royal Branch, where all the champions lived.

Thither they went, notwithstanding Deirdre's continued warnings, now partly shared by Naisi, but Fergus' son, Illan, urged them not to show now the fear they had ever despised. That night the whole company supped together in good cheer, and after supper Naisi called for the chess-board, and sat down with Deirdre to play. It was their last game, and their last night, on earth together.

No sooner had Conor heard of their arrival than all his longing for Deirdre returned upon him, and not having seen her during the years of her absence in Alban, he sent her old friend Lavarcam, the court poetess, to spy. He took a pride in Naisi's renown as a warrior, notwithstanding his jealousy of him as Deirdre's husband, and resolved to do nothing deadly until he heard whether this Irish Helen's beauty still shone as undimmed as before.

Lavarcam was true to her beloved Deirdre, and

with many tears and embraces warned her of the danger to herself and her husband. Then she returned to the king and told him that the splendour of Deirdre's beauty had faded and gone. Nevertheless, Conor, restless and suspicious, resolved to have the report of another ambassador. Failing to get any of the Royal Branch knights to do his errand, he ordered a lesser chief, Trendorm, whose father and three brothers had fallen under Naisi's sword in battle, to play "Peeping Tom." Deirdre, alert as usual, was first to catch sight of his face at an upper window, to which he had climbed, and silently warned her husband as he sat by her playing chess. Turning suddenly, Naisi hurled a chess-man at Trendorm's face, smashing his eyeball; whereupon the unlucky and vengeful man dropped to the ground and ran with his tale to the king, whose rage he did not fail to excite by depicting the lordly, and even kingly, style of the Uisneachs. "And there is no woman on earth," he concluded, "of face and form more beautiful than Deirdre." Then murder entered the heart of the king.

Of the remainder of the tragedy there are two accounts, one of which describes a terrible conflict of three days, the king's hired troops assaulting, and the

Uisneachs defending, the House of the Royal Branch Knights, which had been barricaded after Lavarcam's warnings. Again and again the house was set on fire, and as often the flames were extinguished, though not without a continuous loss of men to the small band of the Uisneachs. Fergus' gallant and only faithful son, Illan the Fair, was slain through misunderstanding by the great champion Conall Cearnagh, who, on discovering his disastrous error, turned in fearful wrath on Fiera, or Fiacha, King Conor's son, who had misled him, and at one blow swept off his head.

On the third day, after a night of ceaseless assault, Naisi, as he returned bloody and spent, ordered Lavarcam to go to the upper battlement to see if perchance Fergus or his men could be seen coming to their aid, but nought was visible but the herds of cattle on the plains. As a last hope they resolved on a sortie, and binding themselves together, the few survivors rushed forth, forming in serried ranks around Deirdre and the women, who were in the centre of the ring.

Here this part of the narrative is spoiled by a ridiculous miracle wrought by Caffa the Druid at Conor's suggestion, but the other and earlier account followed by Professor O'Curry comes to our aid. Evidently the small band was surrounded by Conor's troops and were compelled to surrender, or at least that some kind of parley was being held. "The sons of Uisneach were standing on the middle of the green and the women sitting on the mound of Emania," that same mound where Deirdre had first seen Naisi.

A Prince Eoghan (Owen), a son of Durrthacht, King of Farney, who had made truce with Conor after long strife, resolved to cement his friendship with Naisi's blood, and at Conor's request approached the three brothers as they stood on the green. Like Joab of old, Eoghan offered them the hand of friendship and welcome, but turning suddenly aside, fiercely drove "a great spear" into Naisi's back, breaking his spine. A son of Fergus threw himself on Naisi, covering his body, but whether as friend or foe it is difficult to tell, as the chronicle merely says, "it was in that way he was killed, *through* the son of Fergus down."[1] Then the remainder of the flock were slaughtered "all over the green, so that no one

[1] It almost appears that Naisi after falling was stabbed *through* Mac-Fergus' body, and that the latter also lost his life. It is possible this is the true account of the death of Illan the fair, though he is here called Fiacha (see *Atlantis Magazine*, following Book of Lecain).

escaped then but such as escaped at the point of the spear and the edge of the sword, and SHE was carried into Conchobhar (Conor) and was placed at his hand. Her hands were tied behind her." No need to say who "she" was, though the chronicle does not name her. So, suddenly and terribly, she was in the power of her great enemy at last.

The later narratives rather improbably and weakly cause Deirdre to fall dead with grief beside Naisi's body, but this is evidently one of the examples of which Professor O'Curry warns his readers, where a later editor occasionally adds mere romance for the sake of supposed effect. A vigorous healthy woman like Deirdre, living continually in the open air, does not die suddenly of grief, and it is satisfactory for truth's sake that the old account can be safely followed, as every line of it bears the impress of fact, and leads on through a still more painful and sorrowful path to the tragic end.

For one year we are told "*she*" remained in the power of the tyrant, and during that time "she laughed not one smiling laugh, nor took sufficiency of food or sleep, nor raised her head from off her knee."

From this point the chronicler, with a kind of

dumb sense of this woman's terrible grief, seldom mentions her by name. It is always "she,"—the only real human *persona* in the scene of despair. Other names arise and flit by, as in Dante's Inferno, inhuman, tormenting demons, hastening the tragedy to its close. They brought musicians, but their sounds only inspired the dirge in which SHE commemorates the beloved dead.

Of this dirge, of which some twenty-four verses still exist, Professor O'Curry gives a literal translation in the *Atlantis Magazine*. The following verses are wholly based on that translation, but to avoid the baldness of literality an attempt is made to give them a more rhythmic form, though without rhyme, carefully inserting unchanged every line of O'Curry which scans freely.

> "Though fair with you, the valiant champions,
> Who came to Aven after marching,
> More beauteous they went from their dwelling
> The three heroic sons of Usnagh.

> "Naisi made mead all brimming, sweat
> I by the fire, his bath made ready;[1]
> Ardan with ox or fair fat sheep
> With Ainlé crossed the flooded river.

---

[1] How like the scenes in the Odyssey.

"Though sweet to you the rich brown mead
　Macnessa of the battles drinketh;[1]
　I've seen ere now, the far chased doe
　The food of which was ten times sweeter.

"When Naisi, noble one, would on-set
　A stack of faggots from the moorland,
　Sweeter than honey was all food
　Since 'twas the sons of Usnagh chose it.

"Sweet may it be to thee King Conor,
　The sound of pipes and trumpeters,
　Dearer to me the 'Song Renowned,'
　The song the sons of Uislé sang.

"The deep-toned wave-like voice of Naisi,
　'T'was music rare, my ear, to hear it,
　And Ardan's harp joined rich and clear
　As from the hut came Ainlé's singing.

"Naisi now in his grave is lying;
　Woeful to me that fearful banquet[2]
　When Borach gave in cruel guile
　The bitter draught from which they died.

"No more I sleep [I cannot sleep],
　No more I'll deck my nails with crimson,
　No joy upon my mind shall come,
　Since Indle's sons come back no longer."

---

[1] *i.e.* Conor.　　　　　[2] Borach's invitation.

When Conor sought to comfort her she said:—

"Oh, Conor! knowest thou what thou doest,
Thou hast heaped woe and tears upon me,
And sorrow lasting as my life,
Thy love can never be aught to me.

"That which was loveliest under heaven,
That which was most belov'd on earth,
Thou hast ta'en from me;—Great the wrong,
Ne'er shall I see him now till death.

"His absence, oh! 'tis anguish to me,
How came dark death on Uislé's son,
Death's blackness deep, round his white body,
Who once was known the prince of men.

"Two crimson cheeks of lovely hue,
Red lips and eyelash chafer-colour,[1]
His pearly teeth shone in his smile,
Like brightest gleam of winter's cover.

"Distinguished was his bright array,
'Mong Alba's men of warrior mould,
His crimson cloak in graceful sway,
With bindings fair of ruddy gold.

"A golden hilted sword in hand,
Two spears of green with vict'ry pointed,
A shield with rim of yellow gold,
And face of silver fair appointed.

---

[1] Beautiful, deep-shining, dark, like the coat of the tree beetle, the *Melolontha Vulgaris* of naturalists (O'CURRY).

"Though here stood ranked upon the plain
Thine Ulstermen before thee, Conor,
Without a thought I'd sell them for
One hour with Naisi, son of Uislé

"Oh, break not yet, this day, my heart!
Soon shall I reach my early grave;
Sorrow is deeper than the sea,
And thou may'st know it yet, oh, Conor!"

Her continued grief for the dead and scorn for the living roused Conor's jealousy and hate. "What is it thou hatest most," he asked her one day.

"Thee, indeed!" she flashed back, "and Eoghan Mac Durrthacht."

Then Conor, full of bitterness, laughed and said, "Thou shalt be a year with Eoghan" (Owen), and he gave her into the hands of her husband's murderer!

Next day Eoghan put her into his chariot and drove south with her to a Fair at Muirtheimhne, an ancient plain extending from the River Boyne at Drogheda to Dundalk and Carlingford. On it, at the Battle of Brislech, the hero Cuchulain was slain and beheaded by Erc, for which Erc's head was afterwards removed from his body by Conall Cearnagh! On the way to the fair, in some rocky passage, Conor passed in his chariot, and catching the dark gleam of her eye fixed on him, he jeered at her. "Well, oh

Deirdriu! it is a sheep's eye between two rams that you now cast between me and Eoghan." Stung by the brutal scoff in her hopeless misery, she leaped from the chariot and falling over some cliff was dashed against a rock, and lay at rest for ever.

It was the end of the sorrows of Deirdre but the beginning of Conor's. Like King David, the sword never after departed from his house. Remorse and grief for the death of her whom he had so adored and so wronged darkened his days. King Fergus and Naisi's son Gaiar, with many others, returned and exacted a fearful vengeance on Conor Mac Nessa and on Ulster, driving the former from his throne for a season. Ultimately peace was restored, and large lands were given to Gaiar as "Eric" or "Were Gild" for his father's death, the death of Ainle and Ardan remaining "against Conor's dishonour." During this war vengeance fell also on Eoghan Mac Durrthacht, Naisi's murderer and Deirdre's last oppressor. His two daughters were captured and ruthlessly slain by a friend of Fergus, their possessions seized and their castles given to the flames. Soon after Fergus met and slew Eoghan himself, whose house and town were also plundered and burned.

Professor O'Curry speaks of Conor as a cotemporary of our Saviour and an undoubted historic character, whose descendants continued to be recognised and identified in various parts of Ireland down to the Anglo-Norman Invasion. Indeed, he adds, they may be still recognised, and the descendants of Fergus Mac Roigh (the ex-king) are still well known and distinguished in the O'Connors of Kerry and in many families in Connaught. Connaught itself, by the way, is named after Cond the "hundred fighter," grandson of the great Tuathal Techtmar.

The names of three great women have been placed together in the literature and history of the world, distinguished for their beauty and their misfortunes— Helen of Troy, Cleopatra of Egypt, and Mary Queen of Scots. Whether we view her as a historical character, or as a mere appearance in literature, this "Deirdre of Alban" equals if she does not excel them all.

"*Beautiful as Deirdre*" is still the brighest compliment to be paid to a woman in Ireland and in many parts of the Highlands of Scotland. The poetic fragments still attached to her name, and all we know of her, show her to have been a woman of no little force of mind, appreciative of all the beauties of nature from their softest to their grandest moods; quickwitted, full of observation (it was always Deirdre who saw things first), prompt to act; brought up in a king's house yet independent of the luxuries of life, simple in her wants, and full of affection for those around her. In her sorrow again she rises pre-eminent. Helen in Troy had *hope* and lived to return to her husband's home and happy years there. Cleopatra had many husbands, and none of them was her husband except the one whom she poisoned. Mary Queen of Scots recovered from her husband's murder to wed with his murderer.

But this woman, this poor pagan Deirdre of Ireland, almost outside the world's so-called civilisation, and before the sun of Christianity had risen upon Ireland, reveals a life of purity and honour to which none of these great women could aspire.

She is absolutely faithful to her husband, faithful to her friends, faithful to their memory even to death itself. Those of the Scottish race who read her story will not forget that it is in her life they first get a glimpse of their native land, which she loved so well.

Dun Mac Uisneach at Benderloch Station is her monument in Alban, and the green mound of N'avan, where she first saw her husband and also saw him die, may yet be seen about a mile from Armagh in the land which still of right is called "Old Ireland."

CHAPTER VII

The Origin and Building of Emania—Macha Red Hair—King Fergus Mac Roigh's Death—Queen Meav of Cruachan—Conor Mac Nessa's last Days and Death.

EMANIA is the Latinised form of the Irish Emhain or Eamhuin (pronounce Aven). The fort was usually called Emhain Macha (Aven of Macha), and its foundation, about 400 B.C., is adopted by Tighernach Mac Braoin, Abbot of Clonmacnoise, the higher critic of the early annalists, as the point from whence reliable Irish history may be written. This great annalist's reasons for his belief will never be known, as he died in 1088 A.D. before finishing his literary undertaking. He states that at that time there were three kings reigning in Erinn in joint-sovereignty, Aedh-Ruadh (Red Hugh), Dithorba and Ciombaoth (Kimbay); each ruling for seven years and demitting his power to his successor: the true successor and his righteous rule being guarded by peculiar but potent regulations.

At last Red Hugh was drowned in a cataract at Ballyshannon, near Sligo, afterwards called Eas-

Ruaidh (*i.e.* Ruadh's Water), since cut down to
Assaroe. He was buried above the fall, and the hill
where he lay was only recently found to contain a
great sepulchral chamber. He left no sons, but one
famous daughter, Macha Mongruadh (Macha the red-
haired), who claimed to succeed to her father's share
in the sovereignty. On the two remaining kings
objecting she made war on them, slew Dithorba and
married Kimbay, like the gallant red-haired Irish-
woman she was! But Dithorba's five sons escaped
to Connaught and plotted her destruction. She
disguised her beauty and dressed as a leper woman,
travelled into Connaught, where, after an encounter
of a most extraordinary nature with the five men,
singly, she overcame them and brought them bound
in "one tow" prisoners to Ulster! There her
courtiers advised their death, but she nobly refused
to soil the beginning of her reign with "unrighteous-
ness," and instead condemned them to build for her
a fort or residence. Taking from her stately neck
her golden brooch she marked the lines of the path
with the brooch-pin, and from these words, *Eo*
(brooch) and *Muin* (neck) the fort was ever after
called Eo-muin or Emhain of Macha.

It stood as the capital of the Kingdom of Ulster

for seven hundred years, the province being raised to a kingdom by her, and her husband Kimbay was the first King of Ulster. It was destroyed in 331 A.D. by the three Collas,[1] when the ancient Ultonian dynasty was overthrown to give place to the Dalriadic race who were to colonise Scotland.

But the name of this Irish Zenobia did not perish with her palace. The name Emhain, was called in the Erse "An Aven," *i.e.* the Aven (or the Brooch of the Neck). In time the Irish article "an" lost its initial letter and the name was written " 'N Aven," until now, twenty-three centuries after its foundation, its irregular lines are called "The Fort of Navan." About a mile from the fort, as already mentioned, an adjoining ridge was then called Drum-Sailech, but after Macha's death, and possibly because she was buried there, the place was called Ard-Macha, the height of Macha, which has been slowly changed to the modern Armagh. Any who have heard a native of the city pronounce its name with the prolonged accent on the last syllable, will at once recognise the name of Ulster's great queen. The Book of Armagh,

[1] One of these, Colla Uais (the noble), was ancestor of Fergus More of Scotland and therefore of King Edward VII. Another brother was Colla Meann, *i.e.* the stammerer ; the Lowland Scots word "mant," *i.e.* a stammer, comes from this Celtic root.

dated 807 A.D., latinizes the city name to *Altitudo Machae* as having existed in 457, when St Patrick built a church on the site.

KING FERGUS Mac Roigh, whose absence at Borach's banquet proved so fatal to the Uisneachs, never returned to dwell in Ulster. He lived an exile at the court of the King of Connaught at Cruachan (near Carrick on Shannon), ready to help in any foray against the hated Conor Mac Nessa. In Cruachan, Fergus found a kindred spirit in Meav (Meadhbh), the king's daughter, who in early youth had been married to Conor and is supposed to be the Queen Mab of Shakespeare and the fairies! The union was unhappy, and she returned to her father's home until a strange turn of politics made her Queen of Connaught. She and Fergus led a famous expedition into Ulster, ostensibly to capture the wonderful Brown Bull of Cuailgné (Cooley in Louth County), but really to harry the lands of Conor, her former husband. The narrative of this expedition, the "Tain Bo Chuailgné" (or cattle spoil of Cooley), is one of the most curious and interesting examples of the early Irish literature. It is a strange romantic medley, an inexhaustible mine of information on old Irish customs, history, chivalry, topography, dress, weapons, horses, chariots, leechcraft, and other matters of value to the student of history. Professor O'Curry, from whose works these closing notes are largely collected, says he is not acquainted with any tale in the whole range of literature containing more valuable information on the ancient life which it depicts, and lest the reader should deem the gorgeous descriptions of arms and ornaments to be the creations of a poet's imagination the professor points to the "rich and beautiful collection of the Royal Irish Academy," where "the graceful design and delicate finish of these unrivalled relics of ancient Irish art" attest the accuracy of the ancient poet and annalists.

Time passed slowly with Fergus at the rath of Cruachan. The outlines of the fort are still visible in County Roscommon. Ailill, Queen Meav's husband, was said to be unkind to his clever wife, and Fergus excited his jealousy by befriending Meav. Another narrative in the Glenmasan MS. tells a sadder tale of the queen's frailty, and that Fergus died as the fool dieth at the instigation of Ailill. Whether right or wrong, Queen Meav vowed vengeance and poured her story into the ears of Conall Cearnagh, who had fled from Ulster to end his days at her court. Prompt for his friends, the old warrior plunged a spear into Ailill, mortally wounding him. Turning to escape for his life Conall soon discovered that his own time had come. Three of Ailill's "Red Heads" speedily overtook and slew the breathless old man, decapitating him, as he in his day had sliced off many an adversary's head. Thus were Mesgedhra and Ailill avenged. Conall left many famous descendants, and Abbeyleix, in Queen's County, is called after his son.

They were all killed these ancient heroes! None seemed to dream of dying comfortably in his bed. Life for them meant action and the fresh air of heaven and the sound of battle. To be deprived of these by sickness, and waste under lingering disease, was no fate for a Man and a Warrior. "Better a terrible end than endless terror." Yet, with all the slaughter there is a glorious frankness in their lives and a fine chivalry in their fighting which makes one love them. There is nothing of the savage, indiscriminate cruelty of the later Germanic and Scandinavian races. Women had a high place amongst them, enjoying a freedom and influence beyond that in surrounding nations or even in Greece or Rome, and unlike Rome, women in Erinn might be won or even run off with! but was never bought or sold. Every man was a Warrior, and sought in woman, a wife who could be the Mother of Warriors. The latter sentiment was peculiarly strong, yet under it Ireland never degenerated morally as Sparta did; and to this day, Ireland and (strange to say) Modern Greece, are, statistically, the two most chaste nations in the world.

King Conor Mac Nessa. Like the orthodox story-teller we have now slain nearly all our heroes and heroines, and before closing, the reader may wish to hear of the last days of Conor Mac Nessa. His cruelty and treachery to the Uisneachs was the black spot on an otherwise remarkable reign, lasting during forty years. The annalists, while confessing the troubles following the murder of Naisi, exhaust themselves in dilating on the wisdom, justice, munificence, and vigilance which characterised Conor's reign. He inherited the worldly wisdom and warlike capacity of his famous mother Nessa, for she had led her own troops to war, and no less did he possess the intellect of his father King Fachtna, whose judgments procured him the appelation of "The Wise."

The enmity of Fergus had an older cause than the

slaughter of the Uisneachs, personal to himself, and to the curious conditions under which Conor came to and retained the throne.

To tell the tale of Conor's death we must proceed backwards a few paces, and begin with a certain wondrously sarcastic, but very greedy, poet, Aitherné. This gentleman took a journey around the Court and castles of Leinster, until the dread of his bitter tongue had procured a spoil of presents equal to the results of a successful foray. The Leinster men eyed him as he approached their border near Dublin,[1] nor did he forget that the laws of hospitality, which gave him his spoil and protected it within the borders of Leinster, did not debar its unceremonious recovery by the givers once he crossed these borders into Ulster. Before the guard he had summoned from King Conor could come to his aid, the Leinstermen pounced on him and recaptured all his captives and much spoil. With most of the cattle, Aitherné ran for the Hill of Howth[2] at Dublin Bay, where he held out until the Royal Branch champions of King

---

[1] "Dubh-linn," from a lady called Black (Celtic, Dubh) drowned in a pool in the Liffey. This derivation partly accounts for the local pronunciation of Dublin in that city, "Dear dhorty Doablin."

[2] Then called Ben Edair. Howth is Danish; probably from Hoved, a head. Pronounced "Hooth."

F

Conor came to his aid and swept the men of Leinster across the Liffey.

Some days later Conall Cearnagh met and slew the king of Leinster, Mesgedhra, and under a curious custom, due more to superstition than cruelty, Conall beheaded his victim. The brain as the seat of man's intelligence was valued even after death, being deemed capable of still directing a mortal blow in the hand of an avenger.[1] The brain of Mesgedhra was mixed with lime and hardened into a ball fit to be thrown from a sling or by hand. Conall presented his trophy to King Conor, and for some years it lay like a snake in the grass, neglected save as a plaything for the two court fools. By-and-bye an enemy came prowling in disguise to Emania. This was Keth, the son of Magach, a wily and bitter fighter from Connaught, described as the "most dangerous pest in Erinn." Watching his chance, he stole Mesgedhra's brain-ball and fled to Connaught, where he waited his opportunity to meet and slay King Conor. Some time after he forayed South Ulster, and when returning, was overtaken at a ford by the Ulster army under

[1] The Dyak head-hunters of Borneo decapitate their victims and store the heads in their dwelling-houses for a similar reason to this day, supposing the victor will add to himself the courage, skill, and strength of all his victims.

Conor. Both parties drew up for combat, and the Connaught ladies, with characteristic ardour, still visible in their descendants, collected on an adjoining hill to welcome their husbands and "see the fight." By a device of Keth, these fair dames invited Conor, in accordance with a custom then common in Ireland, to come over and exhibit his fine figure and rich armour. As he did so, his enemy suddenly arose from among the women and placed the fatal ball in his terrible sling (*cranntabhaill*). Too late Conor attempted to retreat, and fell in front of his own men in the ford, with Mesgedhra's brain-ball fixed in his skull.

The ford where this vengeful sling-cast was made was then after called Ath-an-urchair (The Ford of the Cast), and is identified with the modern Ardnurcher in the Barony of Moycastle, Westmeath county, where it affords another proof to the thousands already existing of the strange tenacity with which place-names cling to a locality during long centuries of political storm and strife.

The blow was not then fatal, and Conor was carried back to Ulster, where his physician Fingen predicted his death if the stone was removed, but recovery under a blemish to his beauty if it was allowed to remain. "Better a blemish than his death," said his Ulstermen, and accordingly the wound was stitched with a golden thread, the colour of Conor's hair. In those days all the heroes and heroines had golden hair, teeth like pearls, skins like the snow, lips like the cherry, and cheeks like blood. The rose was evidently not then known in Ireland, and the lily a thing of the future. Swans they had galore,[1] as the sad bondage of Lir's gentle children testifies. Deirdre likens her husband's eyes to the deep black armour of the tree-beetle. Before the reader smiles at the curious simile, let him closely examine the little creature and see if in all nature he can think of anything more beautiful than the dark shining depths of its tiny coat. They were children of nature these old Irish, and, like all children, observant, even of the smallest things of life, which our day perhaps carries its head too high to see. It becomes us rather to admire than to scoff, and to wish with a sad envy that our Pictish and British ancestors had paid less care to that painting of their bodies, from which (in spite of Mr Rhys) their names are probably derived, and devoted their time, instead, to recording the life of

[1] Galore, Irish-Gaelic "go leor" = "plenty of anything," "sufficiently."

those early days as faithfully as the Irish race has done. Let even the Anglo-Saxon be humble; his ancestors ran the woods of Germany, blue-painted savages, when Ireland was far on the road to Christianity and civilisation. At that period, notwithstanding some possible crimsoning of nails and darkening of eyelashes by the ladies, the Scoti of Ireland were a stage beyond painting their bodies; and Burton notes this as a point of contrast between their descendants, the Dalriadic Scots, and the Picts whose land they conquered.

Returning to King Conor, he, like many patients since, was warned to avoid excitement of mind and violent exercise of body, advice which he carefully followed during the seven remaining years of his life. During this time of retirement he must have had many thoughts as to some of the misdeeds of his early life, and the legend connected with his death is so remarkable as to deserve notice.

The year 33 A.D. was the year of our Lord's crucifixion. "There came at that time," says the Book of Leinster, "a great convulsion over Creation, and the Heavens and the Earth were shaken by the enormity of the deed which was then perpetrated, namely Jesus Christ the Son of the Living GOD to be crucified without crime." King Conor observing the sun's eclipse, asked the reason for the darkness, and was told by his Druid Bacrach of the tremendous event which was being enacted. "What crime has He committed," asked the king. "None," replied the Druid. "Then are they slaying Him innocently?" "They are," said Bacrach.

The two narratives of what follows, though differing somewhat in detail, are quite reconcilable on the assumption of the extraordinary character of the events having caused in the bosom of Conor emotions so utterly beyond control, that he turned with all the ardour of his Celtic nature from thoughts of repentance and faith to fearful wrath at the murderers of our Lord. St Peter's sudden attack on Malchus was possibly inspired by similar feelings.

The tract in the Book of Leinster, entitled "The Tragic Fate of Conor," as translated by O'Curry, resumes: "It was then that Conor believed, and he was one of two men that believed in GOD in Erinn before the coming of the Faith." "Good now," said Conchobar. "It is a pity He did not appeal to a valiant high King, which would bring me in the shape of a hardy champion . . . dealing a breach of battle between two hosts. With Christ should my assistance be. . . . Beautiful the combat which I would wage for Christ. . . . I would not rest though my body of clay had been tormented by them. . . . What is the reason for us that we do not express words of deep tear-lamentation?

"High the King who suffers a hard crucifixion for the sake of ungrateful men; for His safety I would go to death. It crushes my heart to hear the voice of wailing for my GOD."

At this point the ancient narrative in the Book of Leinster stops, and the translator, Bishop Finn Mac Gorman (writing not later than the middle of the twelfth century!), offers, as a more credible source of Conor's information, the suggestion that it came through Altus, a Roman consul, who arrived from Britain about that time to demand a tribute from the Gaels. So critical an observation made nearly eight centuries ago regarding a document known even then to be ancient, gives another proof of the great antiquity of the story, and also (under due allowance for the gradual accretion of the miraculous) of its historic value.

Of the remainder of the story no very ancient version is now known to exist, but Dr Geoffrey Keating (1630 A.D.), quoting from an authority ancient in his day and now unknown, ascribes to King Conor an agitation so intense, that, forgetful of the weakness that had tied him to his chair for seven years, he sprang to his feet, shouting, "I would kill those who were around my King at putting Him to death." Then, tearing his sword from its sheath, he rushed out of doors, venting his wrath against Jew and Roman by hewing fiercely at the trees of the wood of Lamhraige. In the midst of his excitement the fatal stone burst from its cavity, followed by what the annalist calls " some of his brain," probably a hæmorrhage, and in that way King Conor died. His last words, according to this narrative, distinctly confirm Bishop Mac Gorman's suggestion that Conor was being told the tale of the Crucifixion some time *after* the event; and Dr Keating's quotation as to the wood where the king died, is curiously confirmed by the annals of the Four Masters, where, quoting from an ancient poem by Kenneth O'Hartagain (who died in 973 A.D.), the following lines occur:—

> "Mac Nessa, the king, died
> By the side of Leiter Lamhraighé."

to which the Masters have added a gloss, *i.e.* "as Chonchobhar was cutting down the wood of Lamhraighé, it was then Mesgedhra's brain started from his head and his own brain afterward." The Book of Leinster (1150 A.D.) contains the same poem, with these lines, but, of course, without the gloss supplied by the Four Masters in the seventeenth century.

So passed away King Conor Mac Nessa in the fortieth year of his reign and the fifty-fifth of his life; a "valiant high king" in his time, not to be judged too harshly by the light of modern days. He lived in the dark merciless days of paganism, when to "will" was to "do" whatever whim or desire arose in his untamed heart. It was no play to be king in those early nation-making days; no time for tapping foundation stones with ivory mallet and merry-masons all around, but rather of hard, bloody toil in the foundation pit itself, with two-handed sword for pick and shovel. There was small choice of methods. It was one of two, indeed, the Sword or Anarchy, and in the prime duty of his country's protection Conor was a true king. If not always a "lamb at home," he was ever a "lion in the field." He formed and led the Order of Royal Branch Knights of Aven, whose renown equals in Ireland that of King Arthur's knights in Britain. In early Ireland the laws of succession practically ensured a line of powerful kings. No right of primogeniture existed to burden a land with weaklings and long minorities. The Senior was honoured as Patriarch of the Tribe, but the Chiefship—the Kingship—went to his junior if abler than he, according to the ancient Rule:—

  The Senior to the Tribe,
  The Powerful to the Chiefship,
  The Wisest to be Priest;

and it was in virtue of his true manhood that Conor was Chief when Fergus was honoured only as Senior in Ulster. No man could have held the authority for the long period of forty years without possessing an outstanding merit as Ruler, King, and Leader of his people. He and his warriors, and all whom he ruled and wronged, have mingled with the dust for nineteen centuries, their very names forgotten save to the few who have loved to peruse the ancient records of their people. If any readers of these imperfect extracts still condemn his memory, let them recall the pathetic line in which the Ulster historian concludes Conor's life:—

"It was said of him, he was the first man who died for the sake of Christ in Erinn."

TO IRELAND

Is thy Harp silent for ever, Land of Erinn?
Is thy day still dark as the night of Winter?
That the Songs of Renown no longer sound
O'er thy green plains, by the sides of thy shining rivers.
Are they all dead? those sons of the heroes of old,
Who carried the Light of the Truth, making Erinn a name,
'Mid the chaos of nations around her.

Bright was thy dawn, and brighter still was thy morning,
Till the clouds of oppression and wrong fell heavy upon thee.
Long have they darkened thy sky,
And saddened the dreams of thy slumber.
Long has the midnight been, yet dawn may rise sudden upon
   thee:
The Day-break will come, and thy terrible dreaming be ended.

Awake! Land of Erinn,
Awake from thy slumber of ages.
Shake first from thy Soul
The shackles of Rome that enthrall thee;
Set the SOULS of thy children free,
And soon from their feet shall melt
The Fetters of iron.   Then shall the Nation sing!
Sing, as thy Saints of old, "GOD save Ireland."

Lightning Source UK Ltd.
Milton Keynes UK
UKHW010658051022
409964UK00006B/484

9 789354 215421